A first guide to

◆

Spain

By Kath Davies

A ZOË BOOK

A ZOË BOOK

© 1994 Zoë Books Limited

Devised and produced by
Zoë Books Limited
15 Worthy Lane
Winchester
Hampshire SO23 7AB
England

Illustrative material used in this book first appeared in *Discovering Spain*, published by Zoë Books Limited.

First published in Great Britain in 1994 by
Zoë Books Limited
15 Worthy Lane
Winchester
Hampshire SO23 7AB

A record of the CIP data is available from the British Library.

ISBN 1 874488 34 7

Printed in Italy by Grafedit SpA
Design: Jan Sterling, Sterling Associates
Picture research: Suzanne Williams
Editor: Donna Bailey
Map: Gecko Limited
Production: Grahame Griffiths

Photographic acknowledgments
The publishers wish to acknowledge, with thanks, the following photographic sources:

Cover: Zefa; title page: Tony Stone Images; 5l The Hutchison Library/Melanie Friend; 5r Impact Photos/Alan Keohane; 6 Robert Harding Picture Library; 7l Robert Harding Picture Library; 7r The Hutchison Library/Melanie Friend; 8 The Hutchison Library/John Downman; 9l Oxford Scientific Films/Jorge Sierra; 9r Impact Photos/Alain le Garsmeur; 10 Redferns/Brandon; 11l Impact Photos/Gavin Milverton; 11r,12 Zefa; 13l & r Robert Harding Picture Library; 14 Impact Photos/Homer Sykes; 15l Zefa; 15r Impact Photos/Ray Roberts; 16 Diego Rodriguez de Silva y Velazquez (1599-1660) *The Surrender of Breda* Prado, Madrid, Bridgeman Art Library; 17l Impact Photos/Charles Worthington; 17r Robert Harding Picture Library; 18 Impact Photos/Piers Cavendish; 19l Impact Photos/Michael George; 19r Robert Harding Picture Library; 20 Impact Photos/Cosmos/P.Boulat; 21l Robert Harding Picture Library; 21r Impact Photos/Christian Sappa; 22 The Hutchison Library/Nancy Durrell McKenna; 23l The Hutchison Library/Tony Souter; 23r Impact Photos/Ray Roberts; 24 The Hutchison Library/Nancy Durrell McKenna; 25l Robert Harding Picture Library; 25r Impact Photos/Cosmos/P.Boulat; 26 Michael Holford; 27l & r Robert Harding Picture Library; 28 Impact Photos/Cosmos/P.Schwartz; 29l Michael Holford; 29r Frank Spooner Pictures

Cover: *The Spring Fair in Seville*

Title page: *Montefrio, in Andalusia, at dawn*

Contents

Spanish words are shown in *italics* and are explained in the text.

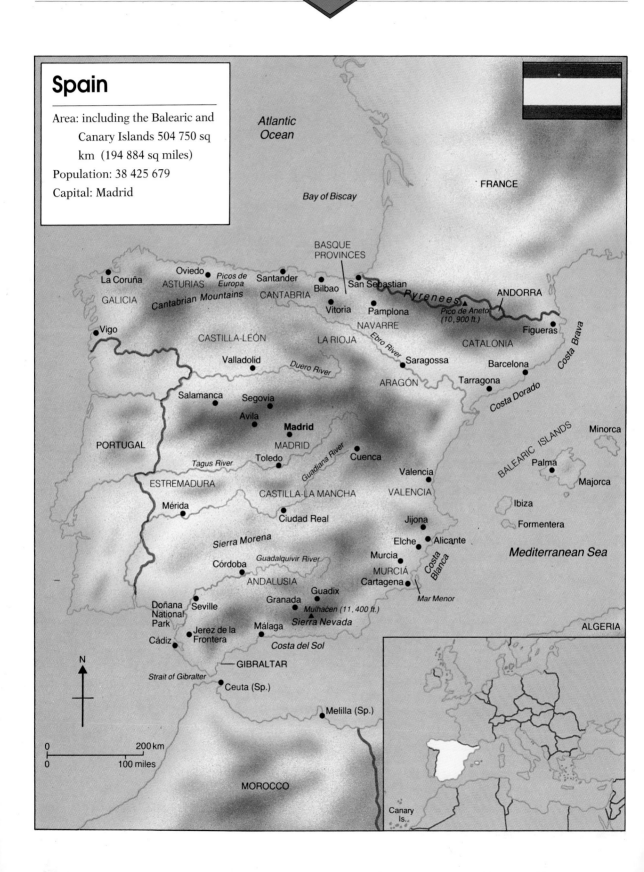

Spain

Area: including the Balearic and
Canary Islands 504 750 sq
km (194 884 sq miles)
Population: 38 425 679
Capital: Madrid

Atlantic
Ocean

FRANCE

Bay of Biscay

BASQUE
PROVINCES

La Coruña
Oviedo
ASTURIAS
Picos de
Europa
Santander
Bilbao
San Sebastian
Pyrenees
ANDORRA
GALICIA
Cantabrian Mountains
CANTABRIA
Vitoria
Pamplona
Pico de Aneto
(10,900 ft.)
Figueras
Costa Brava
Vigo
NAVARRE
Ebro River
Saragossa
CATALONIA
CASTILLA-LEÓN
LA RIOJA
Valladolid
Duero River
Barcelona
ARAGÓN
Tarragona
Costa Dorado
Salamanca
Segovia
Avila
Madrid
BALEARIC ISLANDS
Minorca
Palma
PORTUGAL
MADRID
Majorca
Tagus River
Toledo
Cuenca
Guadiana River
Valencia
Ibiza
ESTREMADURA
CASTILLA-LA MANCHA
VALENCIA
Formentera
Mérida
Ciudad Real
Jijona
Mediterranean Sea
Sierra Morena
Elche
Alicante
Córdoba
Guadalquivir River
Murcia
Costa Blanca
MURCIÁ
ANDALUSIA
Guadix
Cartagena
Doñana
National
Park
Seville
Granada
Mulhacén (11,400 ft.)
Sierra Nevada
Mar Menor
ALGERIA
Jerez de la
Frontera
Málaga
Cádiz
Costa del Sol
N
GIBRALTAR
Strait of Gibralter
Ceuta (Sp.)

| 0 | | 200 km |
| 0 | 100 miles | |

Melilla (Sp.)

MOROCCO

Canary
Is.

Welcome to Spain!

¡Bienvenido! Welcome to Spain!

Spain is the second largest country in western Europe, after France. It lies in the southwest corner of Europe. It is a country of high mountains and dry plains. Spain's northern coast has rocky, windswept cliffs. The south coast has many sandy beaches and holiday towns. Spain has ancient cities, ruined castles and fine palaces.

▼ In the ancient city of Seville

▲ High peaks in the Pyrenees

The long mountain range of the Pyrenees forms the northern border between Spain and France. The Pyrenees stretch for 450 kilometres (280 miles).

The country of Portugal lies between Spain and the Atlantic Ocean. A narrow channel of sea, the Strait of Gibraltar, separates the southern tip of Spain from the coast of north Africa.

Beside the sea

Spain has 4000 kilometres (2475 miles) of coastline. The Atlantic Ocean crashes on to the shores of the northwest and the southwest. To the east and the south are the warmer waters of the Mediterranean Sea.

Every year more than 52 million visitors come to enjoy the beaches of the Mediterranean coast. The northern part of this coast, the *Costa Brava* (the 'wild coast'), has high cliffs and rocky coves. South of the *Costa Brava* are many popular holiday resorts. In the far south is the *Costa del Sol* (the 'coast of the sun'). Holiday towns here include Málaga and Torremolinos.

▼ A sunny beach in southern Spain

▲ Windsurfing off Majorca

Spanish islands

Two groups of islands belong to Spain. The Balearic Islands are in the Mediterranean Sea. The largest of these four islands is Majorca. Visitors come to the Balearics every year because of their warm climate.

The Canary Islands are in the Atlantic Ocean, about 1300 kilometres (800 miles) off the west coast of Africa. They were formed millions of years ago by volcanoes. Old lava flows have made part of the island of Lanzarote look like the surface of the moon.

The northern coasts

The coast of Galicia in northwest Spain is rugged and rocky, with high cliffs and deep inlets or *rias*. The *rias* have small coves and white sands.

The biggest fishing ports are in Galicia. The city of Vigo is the largest port. Spain is one of the world's most important fishing nations.

Fun in the water

The beaches of Spain offer plenty of fun. People enjoy swimming, sailing and water-skiing. Snorkelling and scuba diving are popular in the shallow waters off the *Costa Blanca* (the 'white coast').

▼ The coast of northwest Spain

Peaks and plains

In the north of Spain, the snow-covered peaks of the Pyrenees are up to 3000 metres (9800 feet) high. Further west are the jagged peaks and deep gorges of the Cantabrian mountains. The highest mountain on mainland Spain is Mulhacén (3478 metres, 11 415 feet). It is in the Sierra Nevada range in the far south of the country.

A high, flat plain or plateau called the *Meseta* covers almost half of Spain. It has very hot summers, freezing winters and little rain. Goats and sheep graze on the few plants which grow there. Some areas in the south have turned into desert.

▼ The dry landscape of Andalusia in southern Spain

▲ White storks nesting in Toledo

The rivers of Spain

Five of Spain's important rivers rise in the mountains and run across the *Meseta*. The heat and lack of rain on the Meseta means that all five rivers often have little water. Rivers such as the Tagus have cut deep valleys into the *Meseta*. The Tagus is more than 1000 kilometres (625 miles) long. It is Spain's longest river. The Guadalquivir runs through Seville, which is Spain's only river port.

Birds from northern Europe spend the winter in Spain. Storks rear their young in nests high up on towers and trees.

▲ A wild lynx in the Doñana National Park

Wildlife

There are three national parks in the mountains of northern Spain. Brown bears and wolves live among the forests, lakes and waterfalls of these parks. Imperial eagles and lynx live in the Doñana National Park in southern Spain. Snakes, lizards, wild boar and flocks of geese also live there.

The people of Spain

For hundreds of years the mountains and high land of central Spain kept the people of the different regions apart. Today they all speak the official Castilian Spanish, but many areas still have their own language and customs. In the north, the people of Galicia speak Gallego. It is more like Portuguese than Spanish.

Andalusia, in the south of Spain, is the centre for dancing called *flamenco*. The dancers stamp their feet and click their castanets in time to guitar music. Seville, the capital of Andalusia, has its own dance, the *sevillana*. The town of Ronda is the traditional home of bull fighting. Its bullring is one of the oldest in Spain. Jerez de la Frontera is known for its fine horses, and for a strong wine called sherry.

▼ *Flamenco* dancing in Andalusia

The Catalans

Catalonia is the northeastern province of Spain on the shores of the Mediterranean. Its capital is the busy port and industrial city of Barcelona. The Catalans are very proud of their language and traditions. Catalonia's national dance is the *sardana*. It is danced in a circle to music played by flutes and drums. Catalans are so proud of it that they dance the *sardana* in the streets on the way home from work.

▼ Dancing the *sardana* in Barcelona

At certain Catalan festivals, people called *castellers* form tall, human towers. They stand on each other's shoulders.

▼ *Castellers* make a human tower

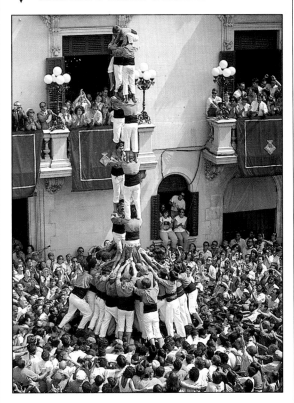

The Basques

The Basque people live in the foothills of the Pyrenees, in the north of the country. They earn their living by farming and fishing. They speak Euskera, which is a very old language and is unlike any other in the world.

Castles and windmills

The region of Castile in the centre of Spain has ancient castles which were built about 1000 years ago. Today some of them are in ruins, but others are hotels called *paradors*.

There are hundreds of windmills in this area too. About 300 years ago a Spanish writer, Miguel de Cervantes, wrote a story about a knight and the windmills. The knight was called Don Quixote and his servant was Sancho Panza. They rode through the province of La Mancha in search of adventures. Don Quixote thought the windmills were evil giants and tried to fight them!

▼ Windmills and a castle in La Mancha

▲ A Roman amphitheatre in Seville

Roman buildings

Spain has been ruled by many different peoples. They left behind different kinds of buildings.

There are fine Roman ruins in the town of Mérida. In Roman times, about 14 000 people could watch horse races in the arena. A Roman villa in Mérida has floors which are made up of thousands of coloured stones, or mosaics.

Water was carried to Roman towns and cities along channels called aqueducts. The Roman aqueduct in Segovia has more than a hundred arches. It still carries water to the city today.

The Moors

About 1000 years ago the Moors ruled in Spain. They decorated their buildings with brightly coloured tiles and horseshoe-shaped arches. Their stone carvings are so delicate that they look like lace.

The Moors built a famous palace called the Alhambra in the city of Granada. Pools and splashing fountains cool the inner courtyards of the palace.

▼ The Alhambra palace in Granada

Two great cities

Madrid is the capital of Spain and is its largest city. More than three million people live there. People from Madrid are called *madrileños*. They work until 7 or 8 o'clock at night, then go out to enjoy themselves. Restaurants, shops and bars stay open until late. *Madrileños* enjoy walking down the Gran Via, which is a long, tree-lined avenue, to meet their friends. This favourite evening custom is called the *paseo*. It happens in all Spain's towns and villages.

Madrid has many squares or *plazas*, a famous art museum, the Prado, and a noisy open air market. The El Retiro is a peaceful park with a large lake.

▲ The *paseo* in a Madrid square

▲ Night falls on Barcelona

Barcelona

Barcelona is Spain's second largest city. The old part of the city was built about 500 years ago. It is called the Gothic Quarter. It has a beautiful cathedral and fine houses for merchants.

The newer part of Barcelona has wide, tree-lined streets. One of them, called Las Ramblas, runs down to the harbour. There are many colourful stalls under the trees in the centre of Las Ramblas. People can buy fruit and flowers there.

Business and buildings

Almost two million people live and work in Barcelona. It is an important city for business and for industry.

The city is famous for its unusual buildings. Some of them were designed by the architect Antoni Gaudí in the early 1900s. He built blocks of flats and a park. He was working on a church called *La Sagrada Familia* ('the Holy Family') when he died in 1926. It has never been finished.

▼ Flats designed by Gaudí

Arts and entertainment

Spanish people are proud of their country and its artists. One of Spain's greatest painters was El Greco ('the Greek' 1541-1614). He was born in Greece, but lived and worked in Toledo, in Spain. Most of his paintings are about religious subjects. Diego Velasquez (1599-1660) painted the countryside, historical events and life at court. Francisco Goya (1746-1828) was also a court painter. He designed tapestries for the royal palaces.

▼ A painting by Velasquez in the Prado, in Madrid

▲ Young people singing in Seville

Music

Spanish people love singing, dancing, and playing the guitar. They enjoy listening to folk music and to a traditional form of opera, the *zarzuela*. These operas tell funny stories about Spanish street life, or retell old folk tales. Young people often gather together in clubs and bars to listen to guitar players.

Classical music and opera are also important in Spain. Famous operas such as *Carmen* and *The Barber of Seville* are set in Spain. Spanish opera singers such as Placido Domingo and José Carreras are known all over the world.

Sport in Spain

Football is very popular in Spain. Matches are played on Sunday afternoons. They are watched by thousands of enthusiastic fans. Barcelona and Madrid each have famous football teams.

The bull fight, or *corrida*, is still a favourite Spanish sport. There are strict rules on how the *matadors* fight the bulls. The fastest ball game in the world, *pelota*, is the national sport of the Basque country. Every town there has a *pelota* court. Spanish people also enjoy golf, basketball, cycling, skiing and all kinds of water sports.

▼ Young boys playing football

Farming the land

Most of Spain's fruit and vegetables are grown on the fertile plains in the east and south. The area around Valencia is called *La Huerta*, the garden of Spain. Oranges and lemons grow there. Rice is grown on the coastal marshes.

Vegetables and soft fruits such as melons, strawberries, peaches and apricots are grown all the year round in plastic greenhouses in southern Spain. Apples and pears grow along the cooler northern coasts.

▼ A market in Barcelona

Cereals

Only about 20 per cent of the land in Spain is farmed, but this is an important industry. Even the dry *Meseta* grows crops such as wheat, oats, and barley. Spain produces about 10 million tonnes of barley and 5 million tonnes of wheat a year.

▲ A shepherd on the island of Ibiza

Sheep, goats and cows

Spanish farmers keep sheep, pigs and goats for their wool, meat and milk. The animals roam over the dry land to find food. Dairy cattle are kept in the north where there is more grass.

▲ Date palms at Elche

Dates and almonds

Dates are harvested from the biggest palm grove in the world. It was planted thousands of years ago near the town of Elche. Nuts called almonds are grown around Jijona.

Olives and grapes

Olive trees grow all over Spain. Spain produces more olive oil than any other country in the world. Grapes are also grown in many parts of the country. Spain is also famous for its fine wines.

People at work

About a quarter of Spanish workers are employed in factories. Spain's industries include electronics, chemical engineering and the petro-chemical industries. Spain is also an important car-making country.

Iron ore and coal are mined along the north coast. The iron ore is used in making steel. There are lead and copper mines in the south. The world's largest mercury mine is in the central province of Ciudad Real.

▲ A factory worker uses a magnifying glass. She is putting together tiny parts of a machine.

Some Spanish industries are very old. Ships have been built at La Coruña for hundreds of years. Knives made from Toledo steel are world-famous.

▲ Handmade pottery for sale

Traditional crafts

Many people are skilled in pottery, leather work, weaving and lace making. In the south the bark of the cork oak is made into corks for wine bottles.

Energy

Spain's factories need energy to work their machines. Most of the energy comes from electricity, which is made at coal or oil power stations. About a third of the energy comes from nuclear power. Spain has nine nuclear power stations.

Electricity is also made by water power. Dams have been built across rivers in the mountains. These are part of hydro-electric power stations.

In the south, solar power is used to make electricity from the heat of the sun.

▼ A solar power station at Almería

Food in Spain

Eating together is an important part of Spanish family life. At weekends and on holidays, families, including aunts, uncles, grandparents and cousins, share a meal. It is often eaten in a restaurant.

▲ A special meal in Andalusia

Lunch is usually the main meal of the day. It is eaten at 2 o'clock or even later. People used to take a short rest, or *siesta*, in the hot afternoon. Today people in towns and cities do not have time for a *siesta*. Dinner is eaten at 9 or 10 pm.

▲ The traditional dish *paella*

Fish dishes

Fish and shellfish are served in nearly every part of Spain. Even in Madrid, far from the sea, baked fish such as sea bream is a favourite dish. The best known Spanish dish is called *paella*. It is a mixture of rice, shellfish and vegetables.

Bar food

Before lunch, many people go to bars which serve snacks called *tapas* with drinks. Spicy sausage, fried squid or octopus, cheese, eggs and olives are *tapas* snacks.

Regional food and drink

Fabadas is a popular stew from Asturias in northwest Spain. It is made from beans, ham, bacon and black pudding. In Andalusia a delicious cold soup called *gazpacho* is made from tomatoes, onions, peppers, cucumbers, garlic and olive oil. In the west, Estremadura is famous for its ham and sausages.

Many people in Spain drink *sangria*. It is made of wine mixed with fruit and spices. *Horchata*, from Valencia, is a milky drink made from almonds. Children like chilled coffee with ice cream on top.

▼ Drinking iced coffee in Madrid

Festivals and fairs

Many festivals and fairs are held in the different regions of Spain. Farming or agricultural fairs are called *fieras*. One of the largest of these fairs is held every April in Seville.

People dress up in the traditional costumes of their regions. Even their horses are specially decorated. Horses and their riders parade up and down the fairground. There are often fireworks, singing and *flamenco* dancing until late at night.

▲ An Andalusian and his horse get ready for the April fair in Seville.

Religious festivals

Religious festivals are called *fiestas*. They are held all over Spain on important dates in the Christian calendar. *Semana Santa*, or Holy Week, is just before Easter. People carry statues from their churches through the streets. Men in pointed hats and long robes lead the processions.

For the festival of Corpus Christi, the streets are covered with herbs and flower petals. People wear huge masks on their heads to walk in the procession.

▼ A religious procession in Málaga

Local festivals

Every local *fiesta* is different. In many places people act out ancient battles between the Moors and the Christians. In Rioja, men dance on stilts. In Pamplona, bulls run through the streets on the festival of San Fermín in July.

▲ *Flamenco* dancers at a festival

Special sweets

At *fiestas* people buy special sweets. *Turrón*, a traditional sweet made from almonds, is popular.

Spain in the past

People were living in Spain more than 40 000 years ago. Their paintings have been found on the walls of caves at Altamira, in northern Spain. They show animals such as boars and bison, which the people hunted.

Thousands of years later the Iberian people settled in southern Spain. The Celts invaded about 2500 years ago. The Greeks and the Phoenicians traded around the coasts. All these people brought different skills and new crops to Spain.

▼ A wall painting of a bison in the caves at Altamira

▲ The Roman aqueduct at Segovia

The Romans

About 2000 years ago, the Romans ruled over Spain, which they called Hispania. The Romans built roads, bridges and aqueducts to carry water to dry areas and to water their crops. They grew so much wheat that Hispania was called the 'granary of Rome'.

The Romans ruled for 600 years before people called Visigoths conquered them. During the time of the Visigoths, the people of Spain became Christians.

The Moors

About 1200 years ago, the Moors from north Africa conquered most of Spain. The Moors were Muslims, followers of the Islamic faith. They brought orange and lemon trees, and made paper and glass.

For 700 years, the Christian rulers in the north of Spain struggled against the Moors, and slowly captured their cities. Two important Christian kingdoms joined together when Isabella of Castile married Ferdinand of Aragon. In 1492 their armies drove the last of the Moors out of Spain.

▼ Walls around the Christian city of Avila

The Golden Age

In 1492 Christopher Columbus sailed from Spain to look for a new route to the Far East. He returned with treasures from lands in the west which were unknown to the Europeans. They were the 'New World' of the Americas.

Other Spanish explorers followed Columbus to the New World. Hernando Cortés and his soldiers killed many of the Aztec people and seized their lands. Thousands of Aztecs died from European diseases. Others became slaves and were forced to work for the Spaniards. Catholic priests also travelled to the New World. They wanted the people there to become Christians.

▼ A ship built to look exactly like Columbus's ship, the *Santa Maria*.

▲ The library in El Escorial

The power of Spain

Treasure from the New World made Spain rich and powerful. In 1519 Charles I became the Holy Roman Emperor. His son, Philip II, made Madrid the capital of Spain. He built the huge palace and monastery of El Escorial near the city.

Philip married Mary, Queen of England. When Mary died, he wanted to rule England. Instead, Mary's sister Elizabeth was crowned. Philip sent a fleet of warships, the *Armada*, to attack England. The ships were destroyed, and Spain's golden age was over. By the end of the 1800s Spain was a poor country, without power.

The Spanish Civil War

In 1936 many people were angry with the government, and war broke out. It lasted for three years. Towns and cities were bombed and thousands of people died. After the war, Spain was ruled by General Franco.

A new Spain

In 1975, King Juan Carlos became Spain's ruler. People could now vote to elect their government. Today Spain is one of the world's leading industrial nations. It is also a member of the European Union (EU). The EU countries work together to develop trade and industry.

▼ King Juan Carlos and Queen Sophie

Fact file

Government

King Juan Carlos is Spain's head of state. The people vote for members of Parliament. The Spanish Parliament is called the *Cortes*.

The government has two parts. There are 208 members of the House of Senate. They represent the provinces. The Congress of Deputies has 350 members. They elect the prime minister from the largest political party in parliament.

National anthem

The national anthem is called the *Marcha Real* (Royal March). Some regions, such as Catalonia, also have their own anthems.

Religion

Most Spanish people belong to the Roman Catholic church. About 450 000 people are Muslims and follow the faith of Islam.

Flag

The Spanish flag has three horizontal stripes, red, yellow and red. Sometimes it shows Spain's badge. The symbols on the badge stand for Aragon, Castile and the other ancient kingdoms which make up Spain today.

Money

Spanish money is called the *peseta*. There are coins for between one and 500 *pesetas*, and notes for 1000, 2000, 5000 and 10 000 *pesetas*.

Education

More and more children under six now go to nursery school. All Spanish children go to school between the ages of 6 and 16. Some children stay on at school until they are 18 and then go on to study at university. Spain has 38 universities and more than a million students.

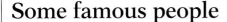

Some famous people

Walladah al-Mustakfi (c.1001-1080) was a Moorish poet and writer. She lived in Andalusia.

St Ignatius Loyala (1491-1556) founded the Christian Society of Jesus (Jesuits).

St Theresa of Avila (1515-1582) was a Carmelite nun and writer.

Lope de Vega (1562-1635) was a priest and playwright.

Luisa Roldan (1656-1704) was court sculptor to Charles II and Philip V.

Pablo Casals (1876-1973) was thought to be the world's greatest cellist.

Andrés Segovia (1894-1986) was a leading classical guitarist.

Dolores Ibarruri (1895-1988) was a writer and politician who opposed Franco.

Federico García Lorca (1896-1936) was a playwright and poet. He died in the Civil War.

Some key events in history

200BC-AD414: Spain ruled by the Romans.

414-711: ruled by the Visigoths, and became a Christian country.

711-1491: Christians fought the Moors.

1469: Isabella of Castile married Ferdinand of Aragon.

1492: Moors driven from Aragon. Columbus claimed the Americas for Spain.

1516-1588: Spain became rich and powerful under Charles I and his son, Philip II.

1588: Spanish Armada destroyed.

1808: French armies under Napoleon captured Madrid.

1931: King Alfonso XIII fled and Spain became a republic.

1936-1939: Spanish Civil War between republicans and nationalists won by Franco.

1975: Franco died. King Juan Carlos became head of state.

1986: Spain joined the EU.

Index